LIMORARA
Emotions' Different Shades

Sea of Emotions blending into An Ocean

Brajesh Manohar

BookLeaf Publishing

India | USA | UK

This book, the piece of art, is dedicated to the teacher(s) who illuminate the right path in life. The first teacher in everyone's life is their mother. Hence, I dedicate this book wholeheartedly to my mother, Kiran, who has been both my greatest teacher and an endless source of inspiration—be it spiritual, intellectual, sporting, academics, or in every other form I exist in this world.

She is no longer in this world, yet her presence lingers in the values she instilled, shaping the thoughts, actions and the memories I will cherish forever. She taught me the importance of keeping the child within alive, even adulthood, and her influence extends beyond me— to my extended family, friends, and all the well wishers whose lives she touched.

Thank you" feels like too small a phrase, yet, Mom, I thank you—deeply, endlessly— for everything you have done. This book is dedicated to you and the indelible imprint of your memory.

Acknowledgement

This book is a tribute to the ancient Indian philosophy that categorizes all human emotions into nine broad *rasas*. I owe a great deal to the timeless scriptures, as well as the countless storybooks, magazines, newspapers and films that have continuously explored and expressed these emotions in their own unique ways.

I extend my heartfelt gratitude to my publisher, BookLeaf Publishing (www.bookleafpub.in) for being the driving force behind my journey into the world of writing.

I am especially grateful to my best friend and better half, Pallavi Priya. She has always been my harshest critic yet at the same time, she is a major support in enabling me to carry out my responsibilities— not only professionally, but also creatively. For over two decades, she has stood beside by my side, and I look forward to her unwavering support in days, months, and years to come.

This is also a special note of appreciation for my children, Mayank Krishna and Pragyan Mohan, whom I fondly call Minku and Keshu. They often bring me down to earth whenever I get lost in daydreams. Yet, it is also their persistent encouragement that has driven me to see the nameLIMORARA printed for the world to recognize and cherish. The essence of my family is woven into this book, as all my works will be. The nameLiMoRaRa is a tribute to our shared journey— 'Li' as Lion for (myself), 'Mo' as Monkey for Pallavi Priya, 'Ra' as Rabbit for Minku, and 'Ra' as Rat for Keshu.

Above all, my deepest gratitude to my father, Sh. M.M.Pandit, who introduced me to the vast ocean of books and stories by generously lending me his library cards in my early years. His influence shaped my love for reading and, ultimately, for writing.

Lastly, I extend my warmest thanks to my readers. With this book, I have begun a conversation with you all, one that I hope will continue through many more books to come. This is just the beginning, and I assure you, there is much more ahead..

Thanks you all for being part of this journey.

Preface

The book is dedicated to the timeless wisdom passed down through since generations, teaching us that human emotions can be broadly categorized into nine essentials aspects. These nine emotions— 'Love', 'Laughter', 'Sorrow', 'Anger', 'Courage', 'Fear', 'Disgust', 'Surprise', and 'Peace'. Countless novels, movies, and literary works have explored these emotions in depth, shaping our understanding of them. In this book, I have curated at least two poems for each emotion, making it a humble effort to honor and celebrate this universal spirit of expressions.

LIMORARA... Readers may wonder about the meaning and origin of this word. When you start writing an article, they say that your start should be catchy. The reason being, the starting of any article catches the attention and attracts the readers more to the contents within. If it is true for an article, why not for a book itself? This thought gave birth to the word'LIMORARA'.

LiMoRaRa which basically represents and symbolizes a family. Family is an unique and most important fabric to have a peaceful society and hence a good nation and world outside in this universe. "Limorara", representing a family, is an abbreviation of 'Lion', 'Monkey, 'Rabbit', and 'Rat'. It may sound childish, but in fact this provides a ready format also for my reader to think of his or her favorite animals or birds, and coin an unique name to his or her book or family.

If you are still holding this book and turning its pages, it means the child within you is alive and thriving.A big Congratulations to you. Limorara is symbolically a very down to earth family members denoting father, mother and two children. This is a book representing a family in an apt way. Lion represents the head of family. Monkey the right hand partner holding together most of things at home. Rabbit is the silent and innocent contributor, and the Rat being the smallest, a keen observer to the big world outside. Welcome to the world of LiMoRaRa....

An Ode to Teacher The Mother

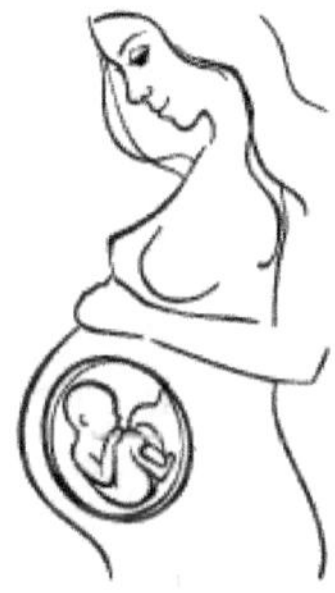

How to speak, how to read, and how to write,
A teacher we find in every stride,
Be it a small society or the vast world outside,
A mother—the first teacher— stands as our
guide.

As a child, you were lovely, naughty and
adorable,
As a lady, you been beautiful than many
other,
Made the family, the society better than ever
before,
Even when old, remained true to all, beyond
comparable.

You lived through the stages of life like no
other,
You aura remained intact, even as a
grandmother,
Blitzing fast, you ran through time, All of us
feel lost, you won.

You cant feel how much I love you,
For the compassion, trust, and love that
makes me is not me, but you,
Creating a big vacuum, you left me,
Not physically present, but I feel you.

An Introduction to Emotions

Who looks farther, a child or the father?
The answer is not tough but rather easier.
A child sees much farther ahead
When sitting on their parent's shoulder.

Fortunate we are for our rich history,
Glimpses of wisdom passed down in stories.
All emotions—heart and soul, thick and fine,
broadly category segmented into nine

Love, Laughter, Sorrow, Anger—
To start with, these are four.
Courage, Fear, Disgust, Wonder—
Becomes eight when adding another four.

Peace at last completes the nine,
Changing the bottle, yet keeping the same
wine.

Love (i) _ I Love You

If not today, then tomorrow for sure,
I wait for you, you wait for me.
That one moment when we meet,
I wish to freeze time eternally.

Tic tock clock but moving pace,
Your loss, a vacuum vast syndrome,
Know' Truth is bitter at my face,
Forever gone, never to come back home,

When I call you with my eyes closed,
You come with face smiling maintain.
Memories are there to life sustain,
Trying hard for calm to maintain.

One, just one more time.

Desperate to feel you, to touch you,
One, just one more time,
You know, how much I love you.

Love (ii) _ Love Prevails

You know, how much I love you,
One just one more time,
Dying hard to feel you, to touch you,
One, just one more time.

Not only here, not only there,
Your fragrance lingers everywhere.
Not just once, but every time,
Wherever I think, you are there.

Aura, wonder, yours the radiance,
Eyes closed, I feel beauty and grace,
The soft sun, crimson red across the horizon,
Memories pass by, framed in your smiling
face.

Sitting beneath a sky of stars twinkling,
Through the eyes, in my soul, moonlight gets
collecting,
Sitting on this river banks separating in
between,
Love and memories river calmly flowing.

Fragrance stays, unknown but pleasant,
Losing myself into your radiance.
Your smiling face appears again and again,
Like the rain, awakening a unique thirst once
more.

Laughter (i) _ Circle of Life

Whatever is written in fate,
They say, will come sooner or late.
Thinking same, yet not working?
Leave the bed, to keep your date.

Take my word, be a change,
But act when the time is opportune.
From child to youth, key is obedience,
Play in tune with parental guidance.

Young now, move out, make money,
Be shrewd or be kind.
Time and tide wait for none,

Keep this in your mind.

Change is the constant only,
That they say does not change.
Still continuing your slumber,
Wise you not getting, looks strange.

Laughter (ii) _ Exemplariness to follow but not seriously

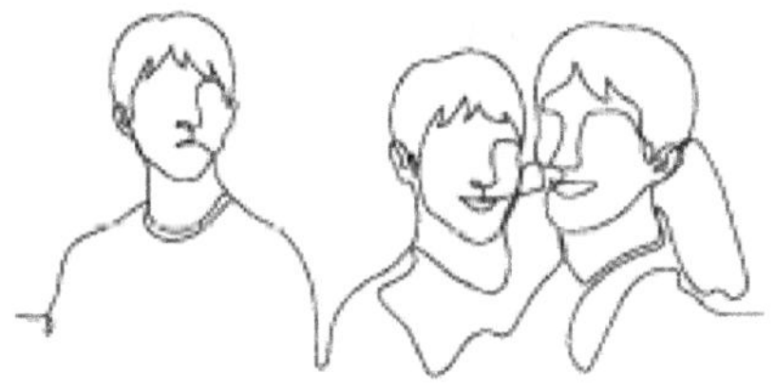

Take the plunge, don't remain on the bank,
Change your position, rise in rank.
Bring in action, shift your status,
Face the world with confidence, not with face blank,

Not longer standing, move n dance,
New culture, new policies, take a glance,
Challenging stagnation, be the change,
Dispel the darkness with your brilliance.

The cycle of change repeats with time,
Be part of it while in your prime.
Admire the Himalayas at your will,

Or sip a lime drink by the , still.

Not getting it? Let examples show the way,
Dreaming to be a writer, a poet, wishing someday,
Threading words, complex in some way,
Will make you poet, writer— whatever you say.

Sorrow (i) _ Pillar of Strength when gone

The reason for my existence, when I seek,
The purpose and aim of me being alive,
Was it only to work only in building nation?
Carrying on this life is not enough drive.

Raising a family, contributing to society,
Paying bills, they say it's simple and shut case;
Running from pillar to post for a living,
Sorrowful inside, outside keeping a brave
face.

Two for joy, when one for sorrow,
Thinking broad, not narrow,
One mother, like no other, missing her now,
As if in my heart, placed someone an arrow.

Questions aplenty, yet answers none,
Status was absent when you were at home,
Sudden death, leaving so much sorrow,
Seeking a pillar of strength now that you're gone.

Sorrow (ii) _ Missing You

You were the answers, to all my queries,
A responses awaited, whatever the inquiry.
Finding when the pillar of strength gone,
Doubts and questions aplenty, the world now
looks eerie.

Nobody else, but only one soul,
You were there, when I needed time to
console,
Her presence enough for any pain any
disgrace,
Magic in face, soothing than any payroll.

Why so early, why so soon,
left all early where you gone,
Wishing for a magic, you to come,
you are still there, prove the world wrong.

I try to go out, when it rains,
more likely to see sky also, it pains,
Cold eyes and warm tears rolling down,
Not confined, broken all chains

Anger (i) _ Console Me I'm Angry

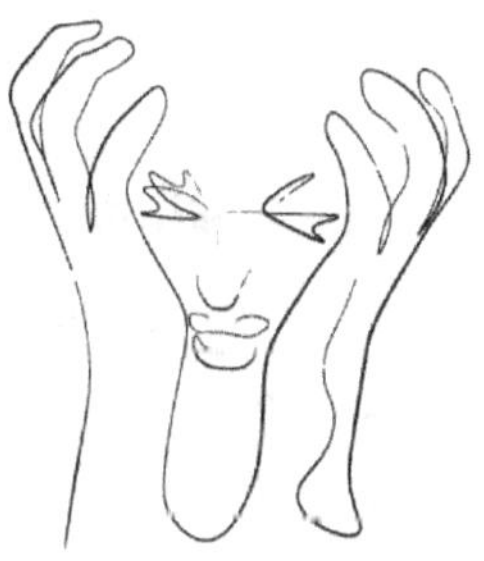

Heat the water, or milk to its limit, to the
verge,
There's a diffcrence, but one must
acknowledge,
Anger subdued easily when milk,
But with water, it rages , so goes the
knowledge.

People preach all day about sense,
"Have some control, don't be angry," to the
fence,
Refusing treatment to the patient,
Would you tell the doctor such nonsense?

Whenever anger strikes, seek solace in books,
Winning over anger, virtue lies in calmness.
When you lose, but you lose by heart core,
Getting the loss into the heart as if a drill
bore.

Mask of patience, concealing my anger,
You don't know me in disguise,
Call me, come here, say something,
No longer a fool in loss— now, I am wise.

Anger (ii) _ Don't console me, I'm Angry

Mask of patience, hiding anger,
You don't know me in disguise,
Call me, come here, say something,
Not any fool with loss now, I am wise.

When in anger, they say avoid roads;
Ignored the advice, I took to roads,
Motor took me fast and faster,
Suicidal it was sensed in seconds.

Anger, anger, when everywhere,
Nowhere to direct, getting it all haywire,
Why this loss is tragic, why this anger,

Burning me inside, douse this fire.

Whatever you feel, you name it.
But revolt again in option
Silent I am, I will be forever,
The loss is also but there forever.

Courage (i) _ Struggle for Independence

Freedom being our only aim,
Breaking shackles the name of game,
See the uprising, the time has come,
Take an aim, and claim your fame.

Remained sidelined and silent for ages,
Time has come, now cry aloud.
Ornaments gone, now be it woods or clothes,
Your mettle is solid, show the crowd.

Buying peace, selling your pride,
All was in past, sweeping all by the side,
Shoulder to shoulder, ready to march,
Freedom's sun rising by the countryside.

The sun is up, morning is here,
Why are you then deep in slumber?
Open your eyes and see the world,
Colors of orange, blue, and emerald.

Courage (ii) _ An Uprising for Independence

Sun is up, morning there,
why are you then deep in slumber,
Open your eyes and see the world,
Colors Orange blue and emerald.

We are the warriors, the warfield our home,
Job different there, we are however here,
Since long we were sidelined,
Moments of glory now shining brightly.

Indian mind, Indian intellect,
Things now falling perfect,

Things now don't exist in the world,
Indians unstoppable now the world reacts.

Come forward, join our hands,
Ready to give, be it in any kind.
Destroying all pride, big or envy,
The valour of Indians—the world can see.

Fear (i) _ Feeling Fear Inside Me

The room is dark wherever I see,
Not brightness, but only a light dim,
Pin drop silence all around,
Something falls, and creates a din.

Embrace me, hold me close,
Assure me I'm in the living world.
Devoid of funds, devoid of family,
Lying on a cot, wounded and cold,

Start a quarrel hard,
or inflict some wound,
Prove to me I'm living,
or living in a dreamworld

Come to me, talk to me,
Do not assume me dead, I'm live,
Or not so it not true all a dream,
Tell me, if in fact, I'm live or in dream.

Fear (ii) _ Feeling Fear Outside

Goes my mind out now, beyond the room,
Out of city beyond the hills, lies a serene lake,
Mirroring in its surface a face smiling,
mocking fun at me,
A Cave nearby opens up I look there, and he
appears.

Long footsteps came to city, planning riots,
Naive and gentle, I threw myself into the
game,
Convincing the educated, satiating the crowd
rage,

Failed me failed the peace mission, got the
bad name.

Got the thrashing, got the wounds,
Not just on body, but deep in my soul,
Mates with me few days back,
Turned their faces, played the game foul.

Dogs aren't barking, sparrows aren't chirping,
Mothers singing no lullabies, sunrise there
Cocks not alarming,
Abnormal outside or inside me thinking,
Night prolongs, on and on it gets going.

Disgust (i) _ An unfortunate Visitor

Signalling me to stop, to plead,
Started thinking of him to be a disgusting creed,
Detailing his son's illness what was his need,
I pondered, asking money, or something to feed.

Refusal from my side, it was instantly,
Jerking small a bit away, persisted ahead on my way,
Shabby in appearance, an unruly hair,
A figure of pity, nothing more was there.

Moisture in eyes not a little but plenty,
Finding an unique force to restrain,
Not flowing out, wounded legs when I saw,
Pity and disgust feeling I maintained.

He was an old man, perhaps around ninety,
A glint in his eyes, gleaming with hope
uncertain,
Limping a bit, hardly eyesight any clear,
Thus I met at entrance an unfortunate visitor.

Disgust (ii) _ Who is more disgusting?

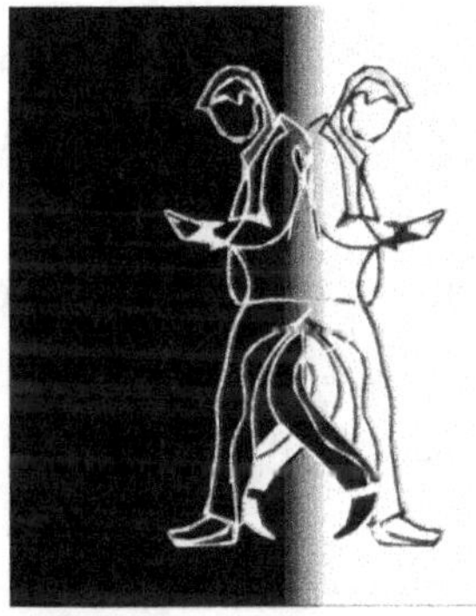

He was an old man, far beyond his prime,
Signaling hope or despair, it was not clear,
In moments of peace, I started thinking,
Disgusting him or me, found the world
shrinking.

Jerking him away, I got a jerk too,
Not much on body much on front mental,
Broken a wall of emotion I realized,
Push however not hard but was gentle.

Tried to disengage, suppress the feelings but
failed.

Started hating myself so much feeling strong,
That man dissolving into sad father helpless
mother,
All into one made me despicable in me.

Helpless body helpless soul, needed help,
Or it was me not him, uncomfortable when in
my own skin,
No anger no jerks, but pity, and I tried to go
after him,
Why a strange hatred on rise for me against
me by me.

Surprise (i)_ Rani Laxmibai and Maha Rana Pratap

Beauty calmness and grace,
With a childlike innocence.
Rani Lakshmibai, with these straits,
Yet her mettle shows but, when high on stakes.

Get the drift of change, drastic and insane,
Bravery, valor brings then her alter face,
When intense goes on field the battle cries,
Enemies before her nothing but, small fries.

Chapter changes, changed now name,
Maha Rana Pratap steps into frame.
Chetak, his horse, not a wind but a hurricane,
Galloping on fields, feelings these trend.

Rana thinking of river in front big spread,
How to cross it, and move ahead.
Before the thoughts of Rana concluded,
Chetak covered the stretch, leaving trail of
dust behind.

Surprise (ii) _ India and Indians Surprising the World

Student— bright, brilliant, and young,
Courage and determination define Bhagat
Singh.
Name itself spells the dignified valour,
Going without fear to the sacrificial altar.

A freedom fighter par excellence,
Not running out but he surrenders boldly,
Surrender inside causing explosions in brains
outside,
Youth even now draws inspiration closely.

Comes the year now, we are young,
We the youth, speed, mettle, intel everywhere,
breathing fire, Indoor outdoor everywhere
Here comes the new gen, doors to open flung.

World around to see and feel,
To act and part ways to pave the way,
The way leading the throne lying there,
We, the Indians, are reaching there.

Peace (i) _ Peace of Mind

Peace of mind, you try to define,
Not easy, but very tough,
Changes definition with person,
The road not easy but very rough.

A village serene at a countryside,
Calm and slow gets its beauty there,
Muddy pathways going to fields,
Smiling children running here.

Thinking of this scene again and again
Fills your heart n mind with peaceful gain,
Smiling footsteps when enter the home,
Peaceful thoughts breaking chain.

Outside when peace joy n laughter abound,
Calm, serene and happy faces all around,

Depending on the atmosphere surrounding
outside,
Peace of mind even disturbed, comes back
around.

Peace (ii) _ Peace in the City

Big city, metro city, calm and quite,
A well lit room, pen and paper to write,
Is this not peace then what it is,
Asking the poet with his face bright.

The loudness of silence, awakens me silently,
Seriously thinking of yours poor condition,
Gentle and cool breeze outside,
Not better than regulated air conditioning
inside.

It is now years together,
Looking for peace here and there,
World of me inside paper, inside books,
Limited to this world peace real not there.

Someone at the door, a promising guide,
Knock promising real peace to be explained,
Fear of exposure inhibiting self,
Opening the door not, inside me remained.

Plunging deeper n deeper to the peace it is
People say, real peace is in flying high,
running outside,
Chaos ends and comes the peace of mind they
say,
But what they fail to see is the burial of
dreams inside.

An End to an Odyssey

Close to heart, dear and near,
Want to stay with us forever.
Beginning with an end in mind,
And starting afresh for a new endeavor.

A trip to air, from the earth,
Rising to sky seeking its worth,
Kissing clouds, one and the other,
Dancing feather like, up and down, back and
forth.

Hopping onto a yacht, set the sailor,
One sea to another and then another
Sea of emotions changing hues and colors,
Drenching in emotions, pleasure forever.

A journey started with emotions in air,
Words on pen, paper, typewriter, or
computer,
Closing a door, to open another,
End of an odyssey, for a poetry lover.

www.ingramcontent.com/pod-product-compliance
Lightning Source LLC
La Vergne TN
LVHW021250200726
843509LV00012B/1622